HOW CAN MY EYES SEE?
SIGHT AND THE EYE

**Biology 1st Grade
Children's Biology Books**

Speedy Publishing LLC

40 E. Main St. #1156

Newark, DE 19711

www.speedypublishing.com

Copyright 2017

All Rights reserved. No part of this book may be reproduced or used in any way or form or by any means whether electronic or mechanical, this means that you cannot record or photocopy any material ideas or tips that are provided in this book

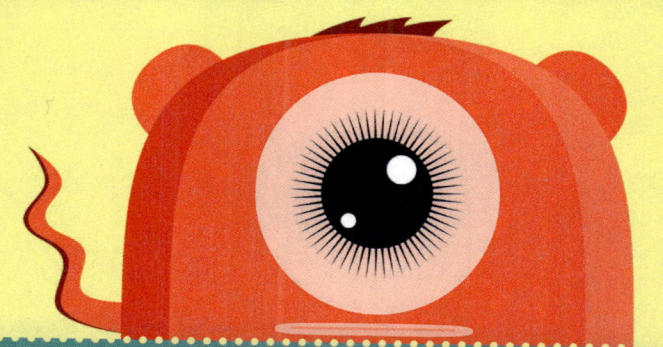

In this book, we're going to talk about how your eyes see. So, let's get right to it!

Which organ in your body lets you see the colors of flowers in a garden? Which part helps you read a computer screen? Which part makes tears when you are watching a sad movie? Which organ has muscles that can adjust to objects that are close and those that are far away?

If you guessed your eyes, then you're right! Your eyes are amazing visual organs that work all day for you. When you first wake up in the morning, you might rub your eyes a little to get them to wake up. After they do, they work from morning until you take a nap or go to sleep at night.

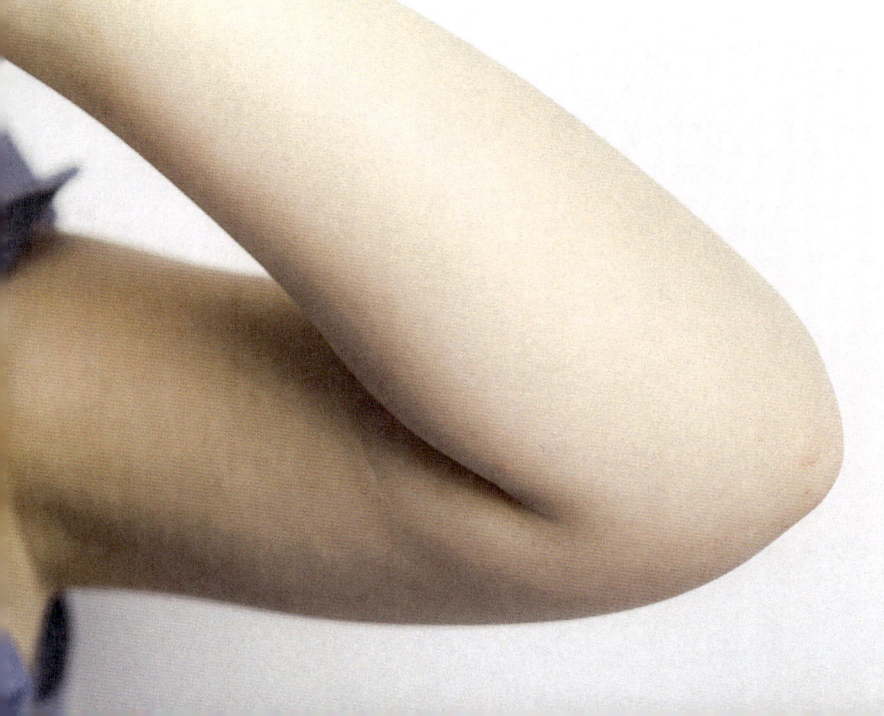

THE STRUCTURE OF THE EYE

If you've ever seen a skull, then you know how an eye socket looks. There are two hollow eye sockets in your skull and this is where your eyes are located. They are the size of ping-pong balls. You can't see the entire structure of your eye, just the front part of it.

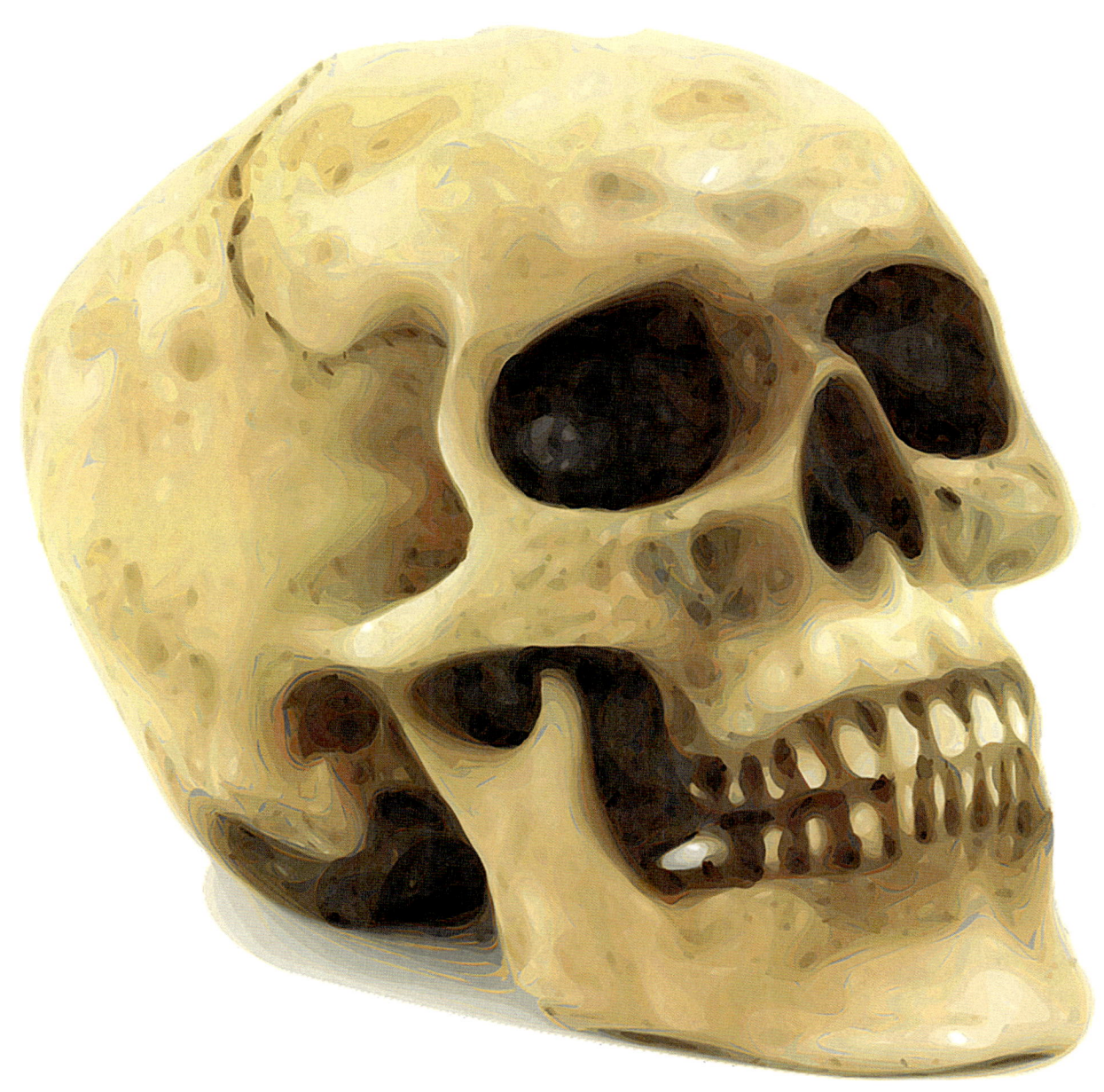
A Human Skull

Child's Eyelid

THE EYELIDS

Your eyelids help to keep your eyes safe. If something flies toward your face, your eyelids will automatically close to protect the delicate surface of your eyes. Your eyelids blink 15-20 times per minute. Blinking helps your eyes stay clean and moist. Scientists have also found that blinking gives your brain a rest from processing everything that's going on around you.

Your eyelids blink without you thinking about it, but you can also blink if you make yourself blink. Blinking is involuntary when you're not thinking about it and it happens automatically. It's voluntary when you do it on purpose. Your eyelashes help too. They keep dust and pollen out of your eyes.

Sclera the eyeball's white part.

THE SCLERA

The eyeball's white part is the sclera. If you look closely at it, you'll see very tiny blood vessels that bring blood to the sclera. If your eyes are bloodshot, these pink blood vessels will look red and irritated. The white of your eye protects your eyeball and is composed of tough tissue.

Out of 633 different types of primates, which are animals like humans, humans are the only ones that have whites in their eyes. Scientists think this is because humans have evolved to talk with each other in large groups.

You can see where someone else is looking if you watch his eyes. And, if someone rolls his eyes at you, you'll know he's annoyed even if he hasn't said so!

A contact lens is placed on the cornea.

THE CORNEA

A clear dome sits on top of the colored part of your eye. It's called the cornea. As rays of light come through your eye, the cornea's rounded surface bends the light rays so they will be focused as they come into your eye. It's hard to see your cornea since the tissue it's made of is clear.

THE IRIS

Underneath the clear cornea of your eye is the colorful part of your eye. It's called the iris. When we say that a person has brown eyes or blue eyes, we're talking about this part of the eye, not the whole eye. The iris contains muscles that change its size.

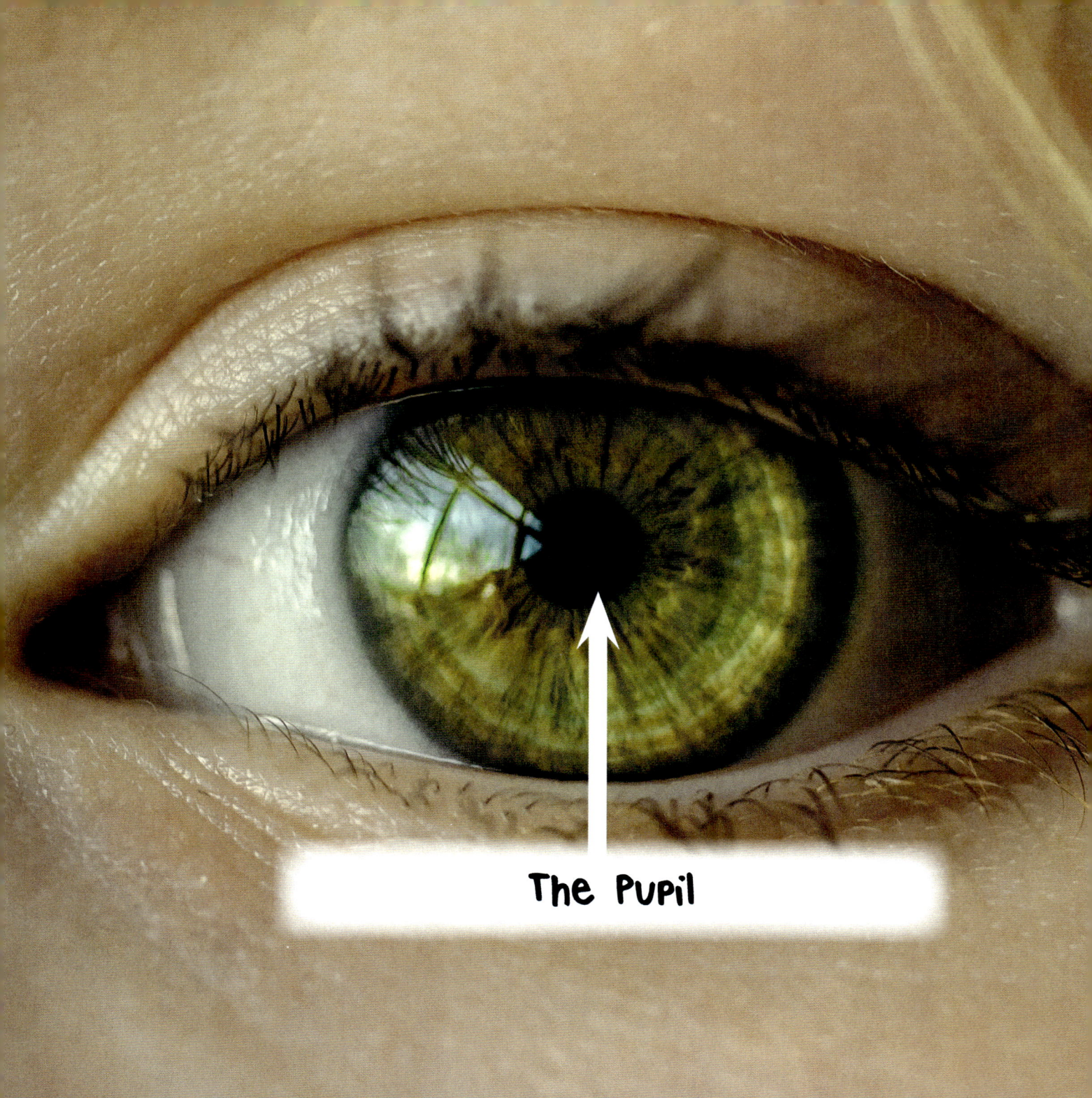
The Pupil

THE PUPIL

The pupil is the black hole in the center of the colored part of your eye. This black hole lets light come into your eye. Your iris controls the amount of light that gets into your pupil.

A pupil in the light.

If it's very bright, the pupil gets smaller and if it's very dark the pupil gets larger so more light will get into your eye. Another time you may have noticed this change in your pupil

A pupil in the dark.

is when the eye doctor puts drops into your eyes. These drops dilate your pupils, which means they make your pupils larger so that the doctor can look inside your eyes.

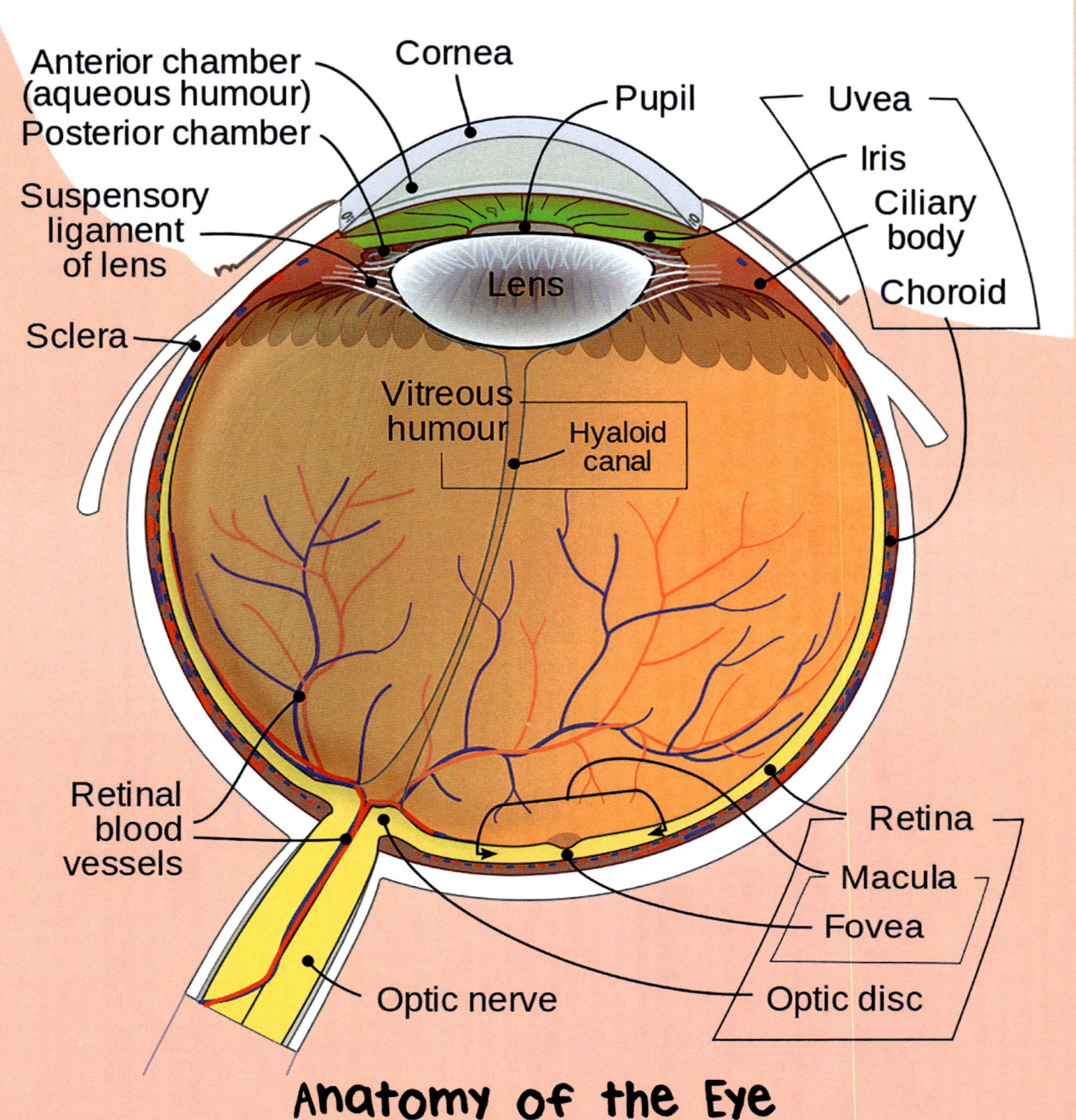

THE ANTERIOR CHAMBER

The cornea and the iris have some space between them. This space is called the anterior chamber. It has a special clear fluid that keeps your eye healthy.

THE LENS

The lens and other parts of your eye are located behind the pupil and iris so you can't see them yourself if you look in a mirror. The lens is located behind the pupil and iris and it is clear. Its job is to gather up the light rays streaming through your pupil and to focus them on the very back of your part of your eye.

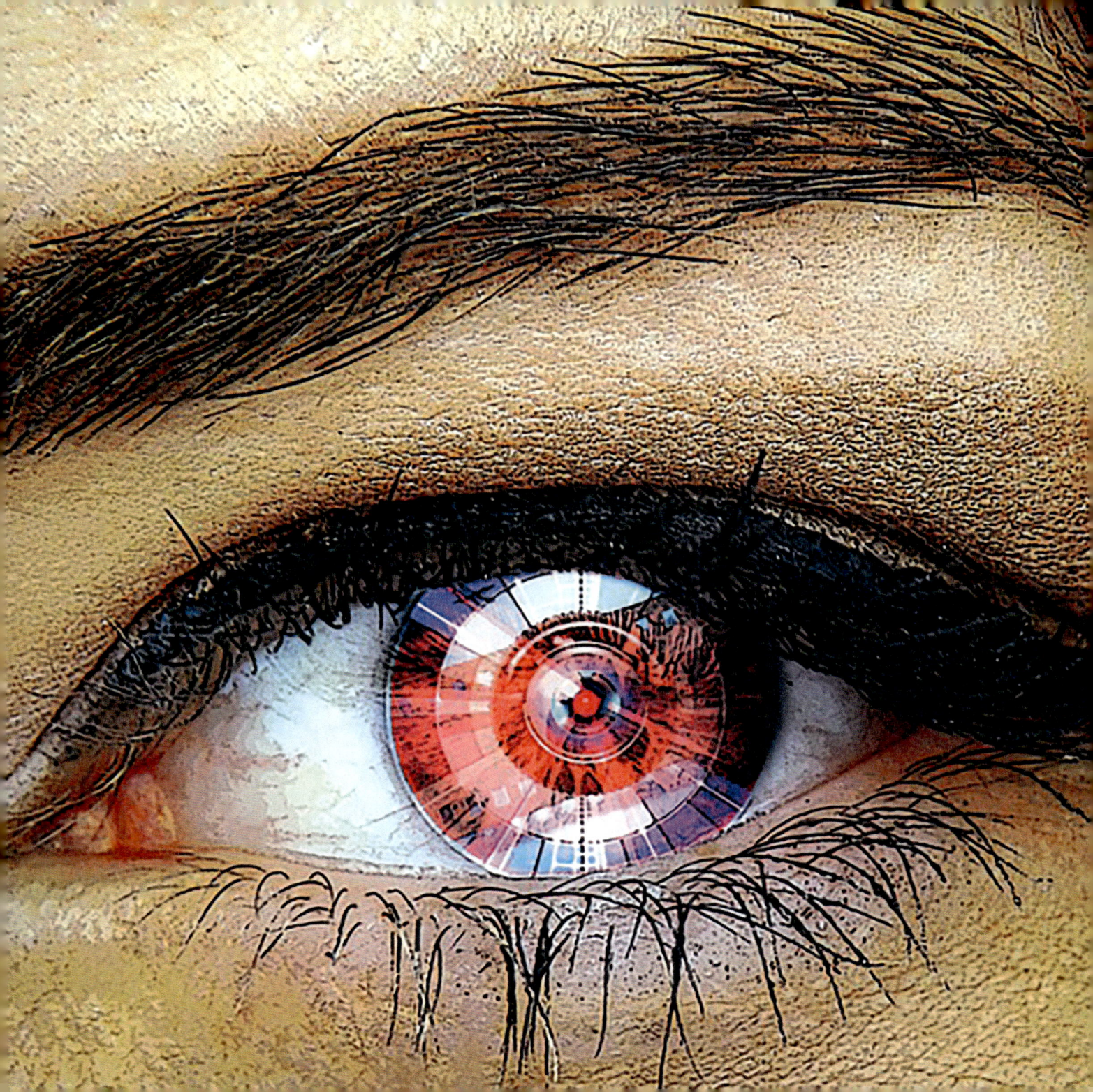

Through the use of special muscles, the lens changes shape within your eye. You don't feel this change, but it happens all that time as you refocus your eyes from an object that's close to an object that's far away. Cameras, telescopes, and projectors all have manmade lenses that work in a similar way.

THE RETINA

Once the image is focused and projected on to the retina, the retina's job begins. It contains millions of light-sensitive cells. These cells receive the image created by the light and change it into nerve impulses so your brain can figure out what you're seeing.

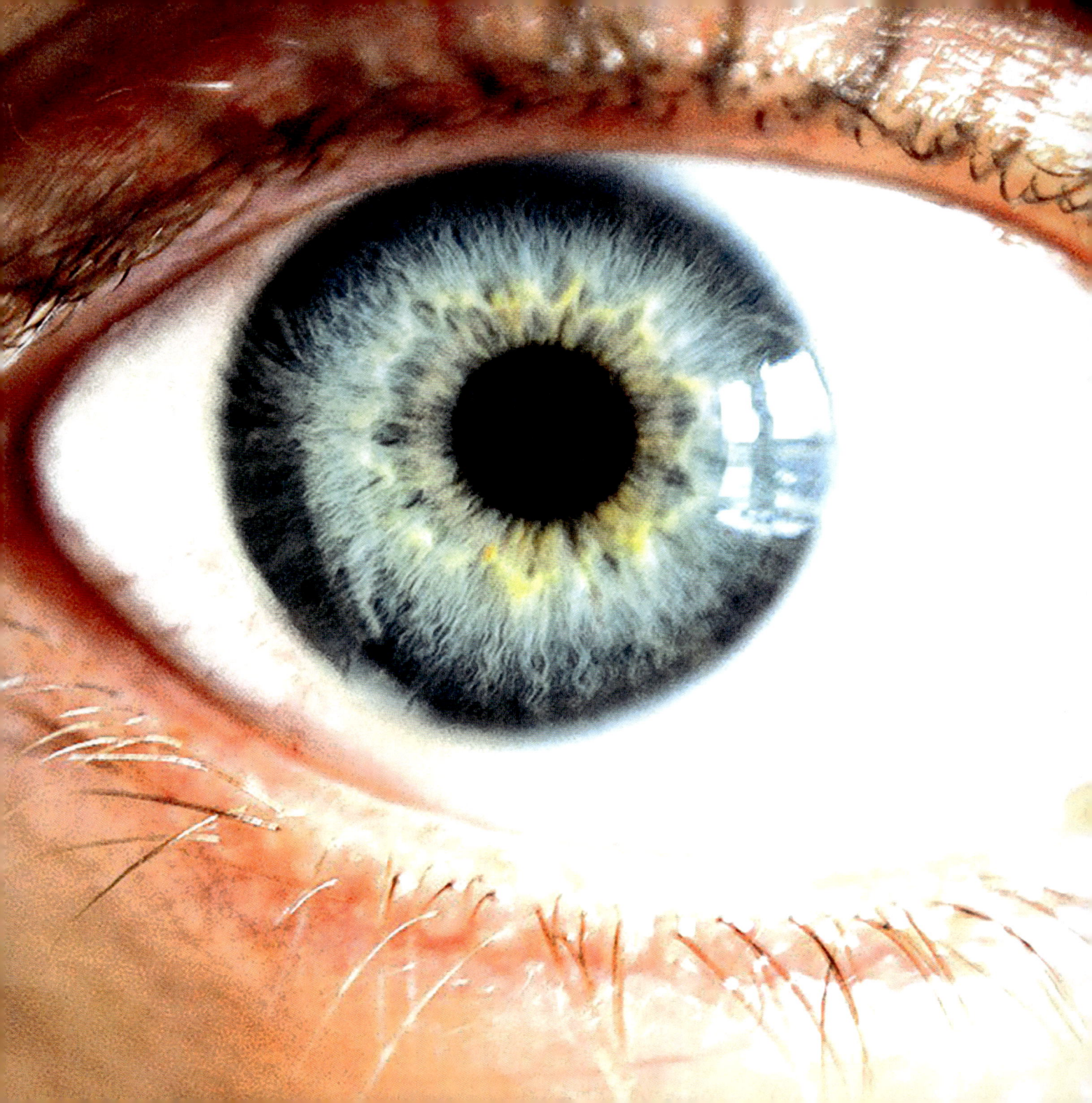

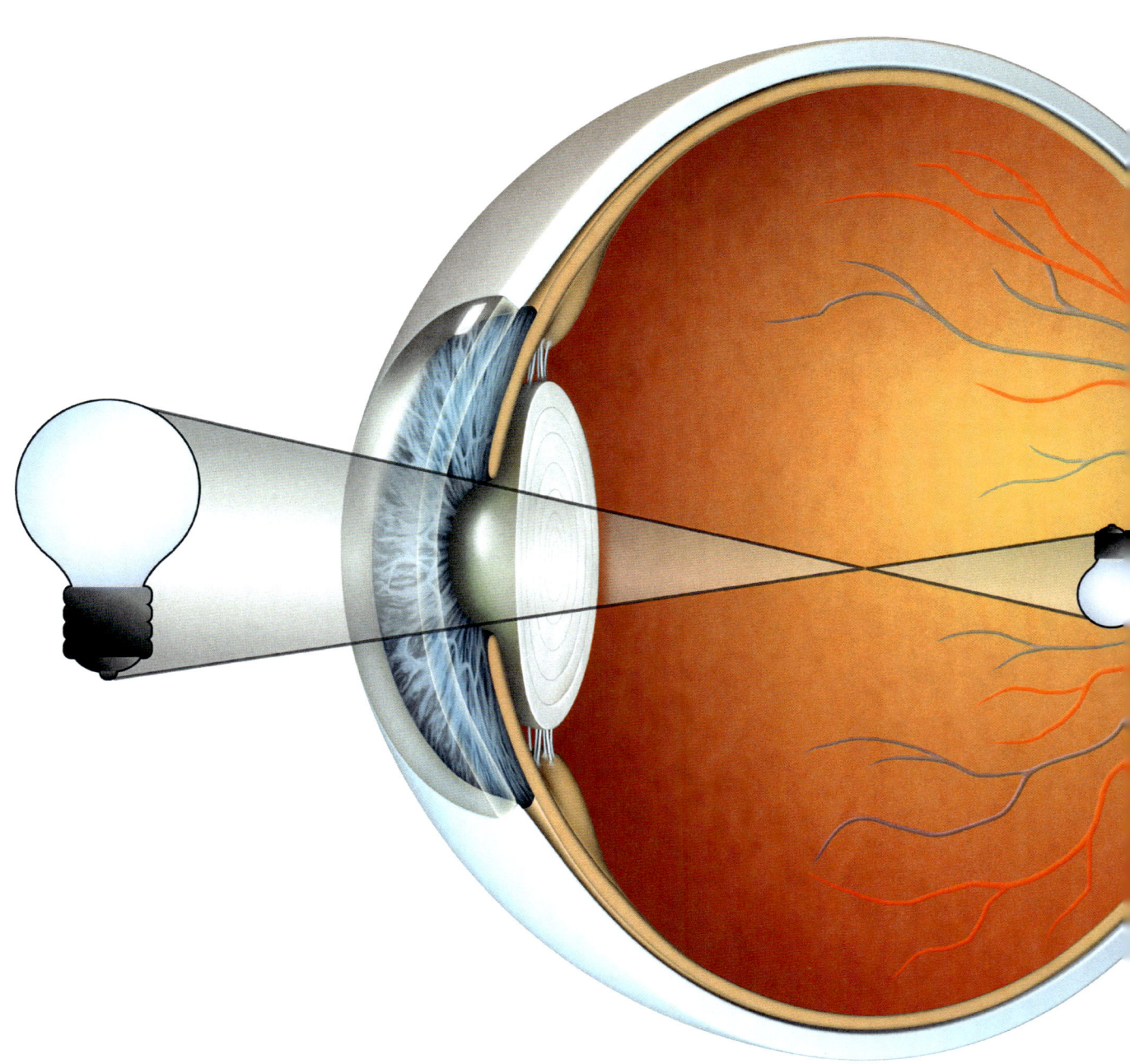

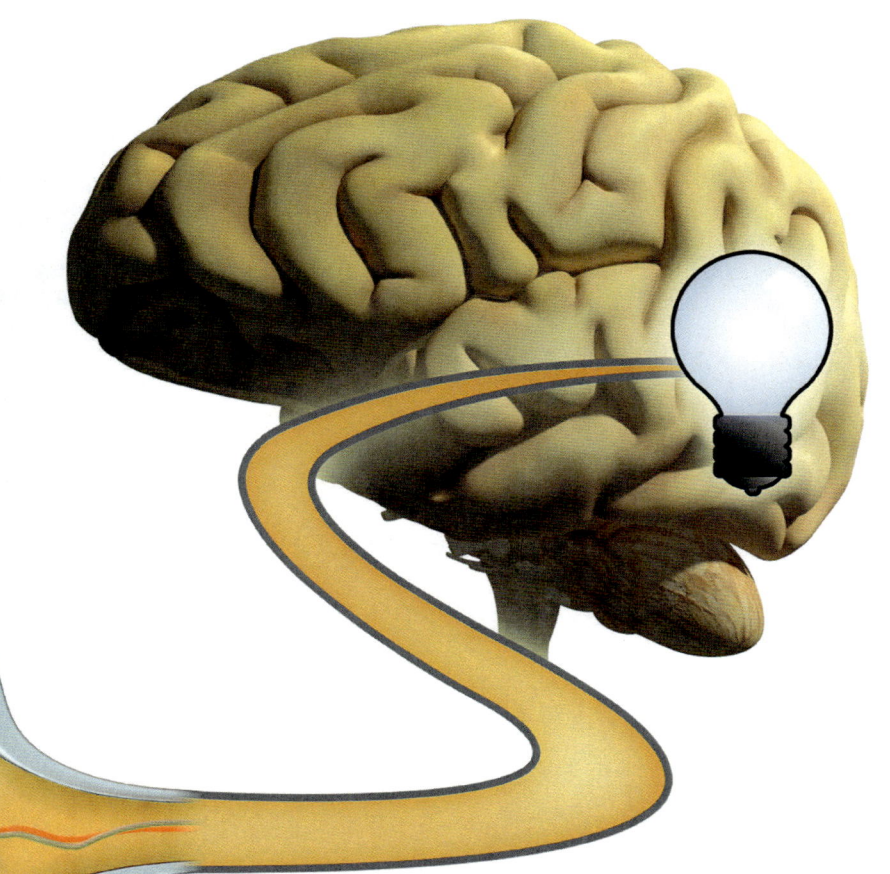

T he image that the lens projects on to your retina is actually upside down! The brain figures this out though, so that you don't see everything upside down from the way it actually is.

THE CILIARY MUSCLE

A group of tissues like fibers hold the lens of your eye in position. Attached to these fibers there's a muscle. This is the ciliary muscle and its job is to alter the shape of your eye's lens.

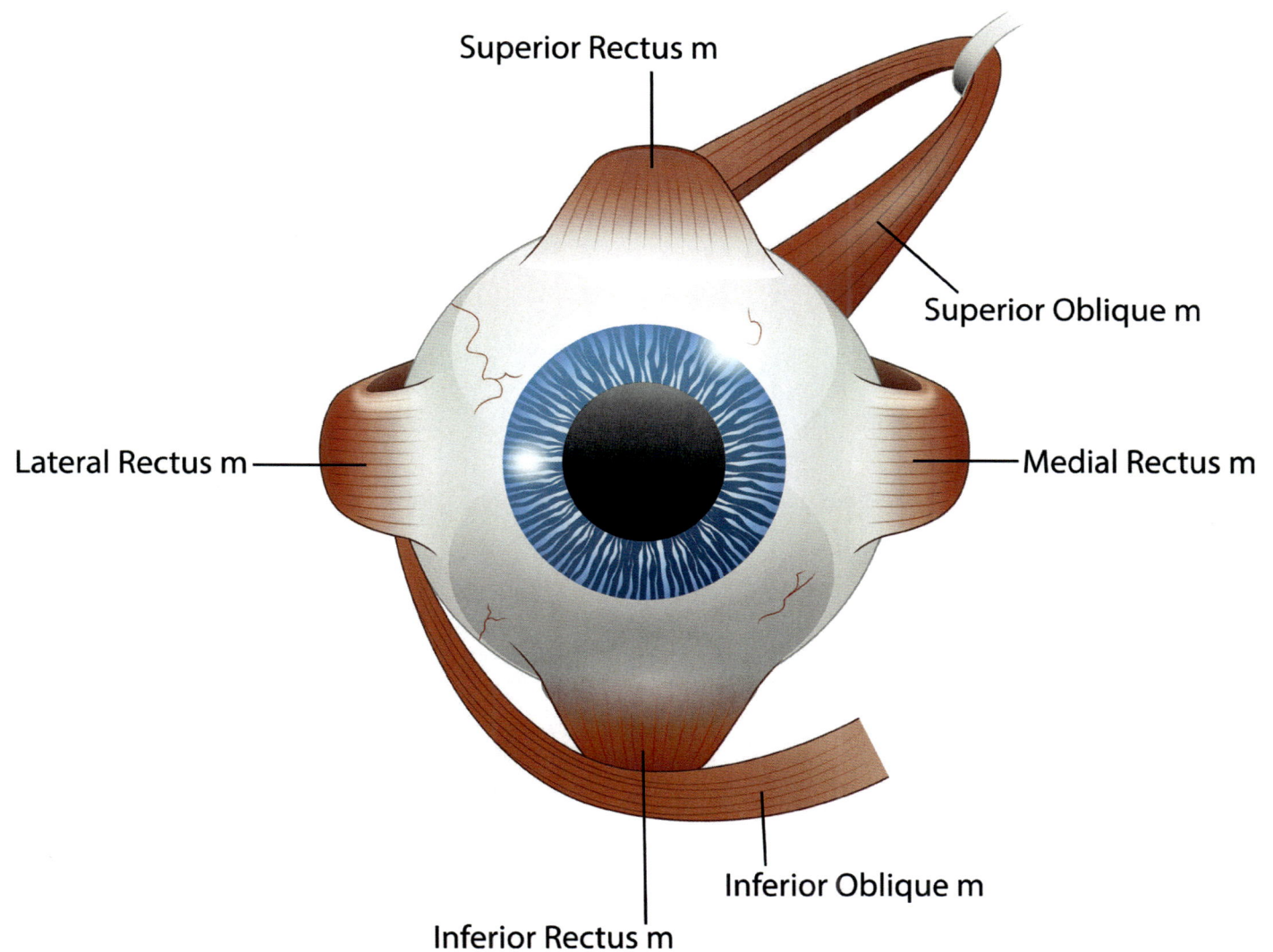

When you're looking at an object very close, the ciliary muscle reshapes your lens so that it's thicker. When the object is far away, this muscle reshapes your lens so it's thinner. If you don't have perfect vision, your eyeglasses or contact lenses correct your vision so that you can see close as well as far away.

THE VITREOUS BODY

Have you ever felt a squishy toy like a Halloween eyeball? It's made of a material that moves like jelly. Your real eyeball is like the toy one. The vitreous body is located behind the lens of your eye.

A squishy eye ball

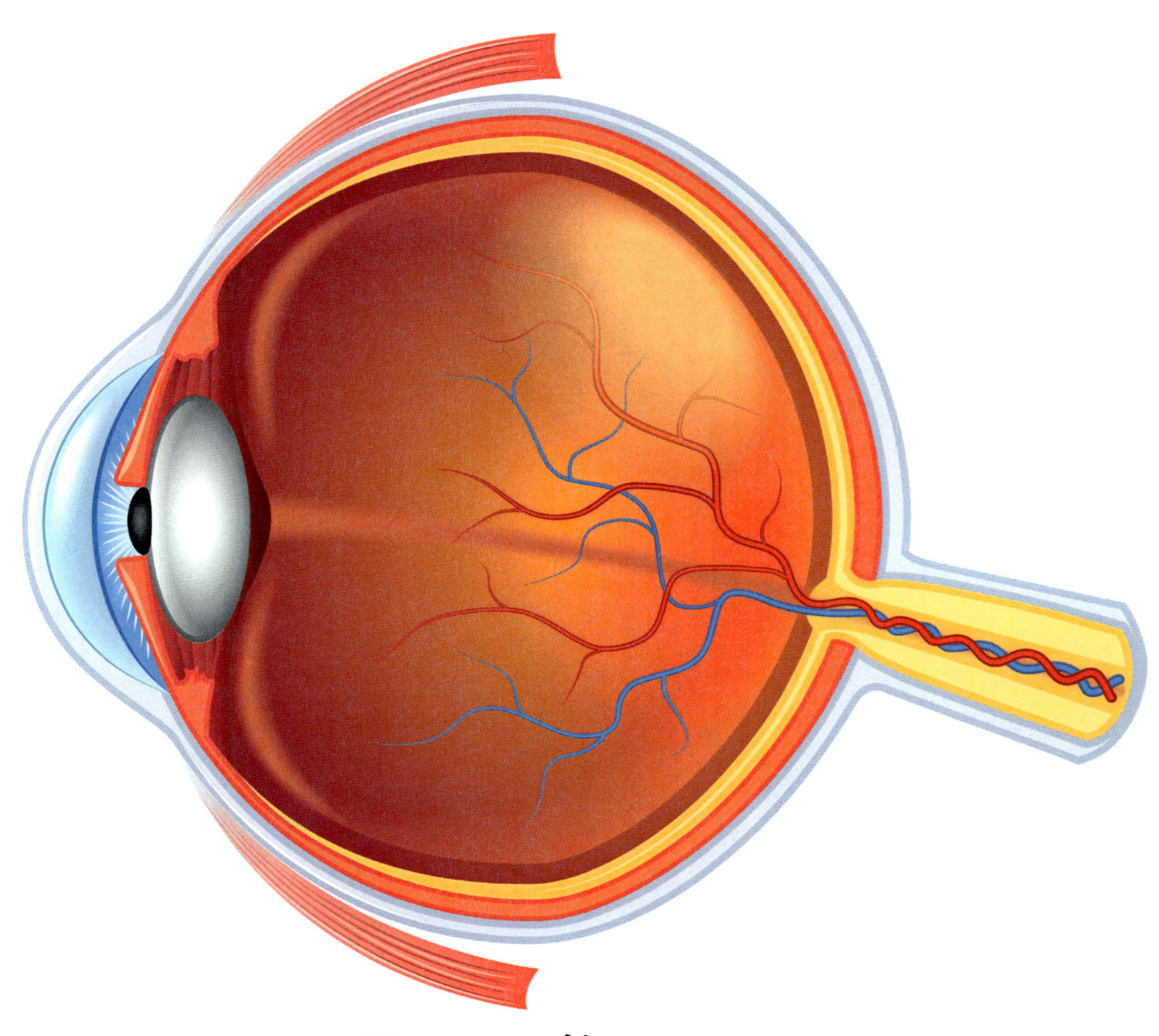

Vitreous Humor

It's the biggest part of your eye's structure, about two-thirds of it. It holds a clear material that has a strange name—the vitreous humor. When light passes through your eye's lens, it passes through this jelly-like material to get to the back of your eye.

RODS AND CONES

Your retina is filled with millions of cells that help you see shades and colors. Rods are the cells that help you see shapes. They can transmit contrasts in black and white and also shades of gray. Even when it's very dark in a room, these cells help us make out shapes so we don't run into a piece of furniture.

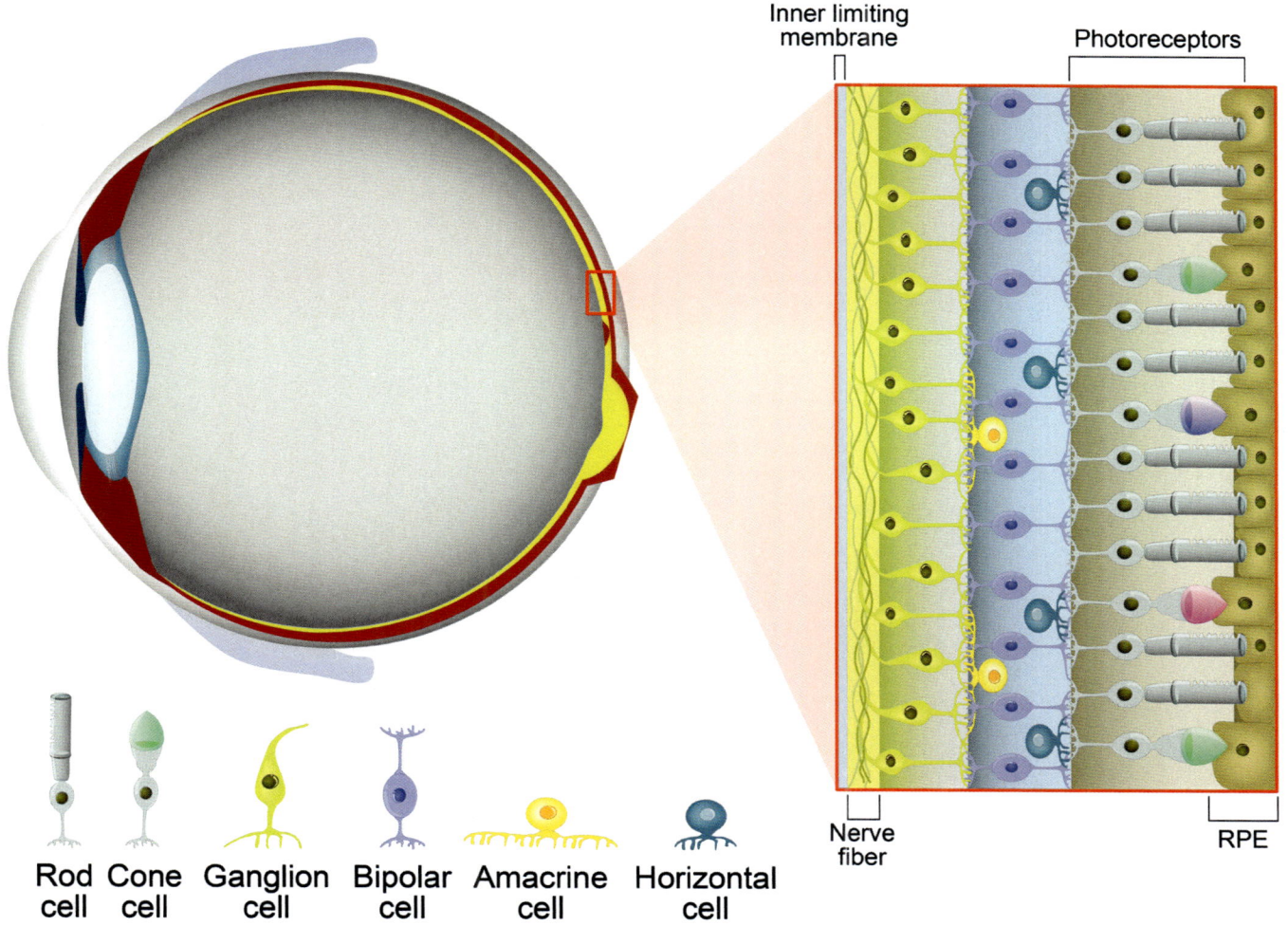

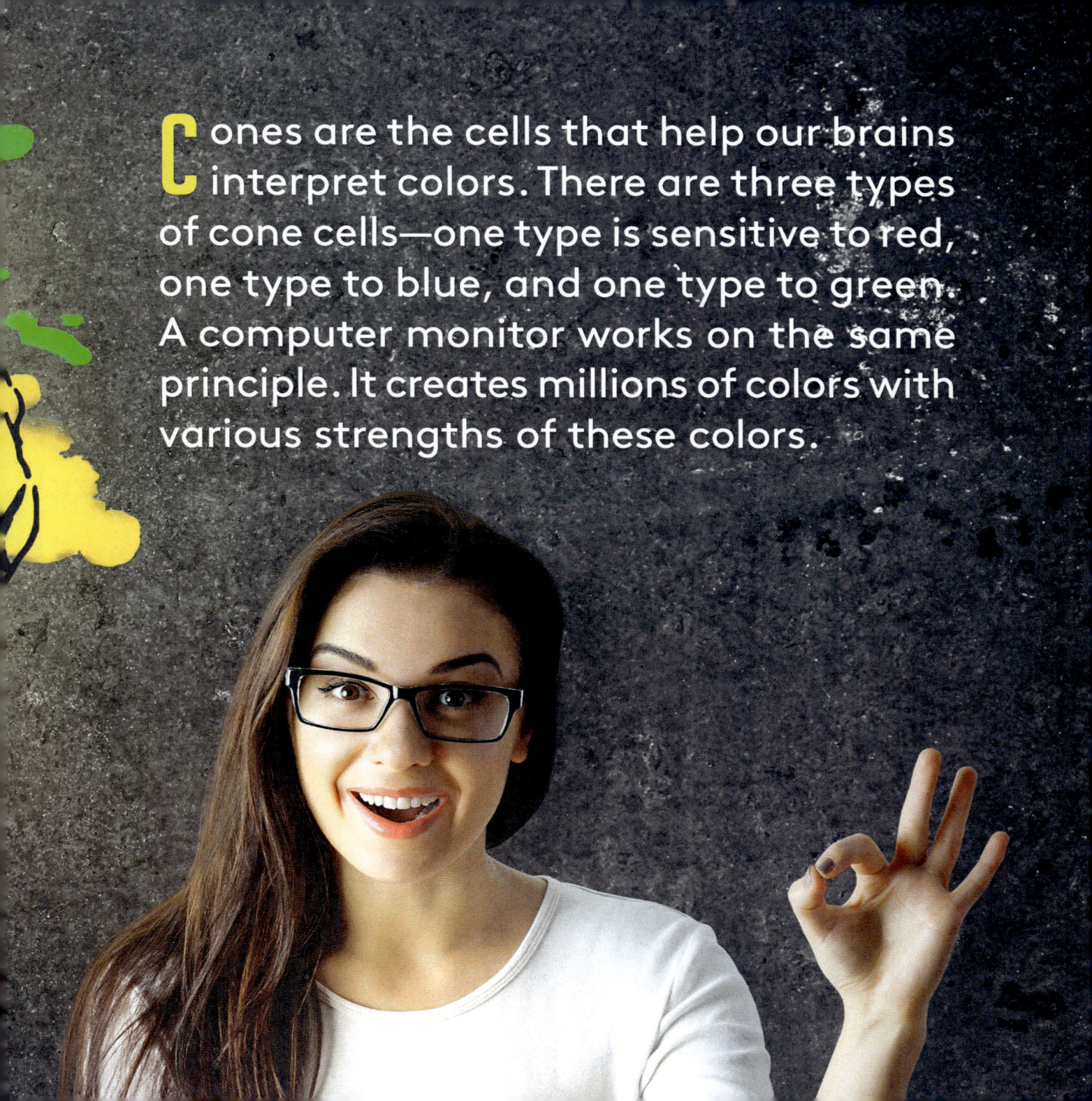

Cones are the cells that help our brains interpret colors. There are three types of cone cells—one type is sensitive to red, one type to blue, and one type to green. A computer monitor works on the same principle. It creates millions of colors with various strengths of these colors.

Each of your eyes has rods and cones. Scientists estimate that the number of rods is around 120 million and the number of cones is around 7 million. Those are the numbers of cells in each eye! Unless you are color blind, you'll be able to see millions of different colors. Human eyes can't see all colors though.

There are also some people who are color blind, which simply means that they can't distinguish some colors from others. About 8% of all men and less than 1% of women have some form of color blindness. Some animals can see colors we can't see. For example, hummingbirds can see ultraviolet light, so colors look different to them.

DEPTH PERCEPTION

When we look at something, each eye gives us a picture that's not exactly the same. Our mind blends what we are seeing into one image. The way we see helps us figure out how far away objects are from each other. This ability is our depth perception.

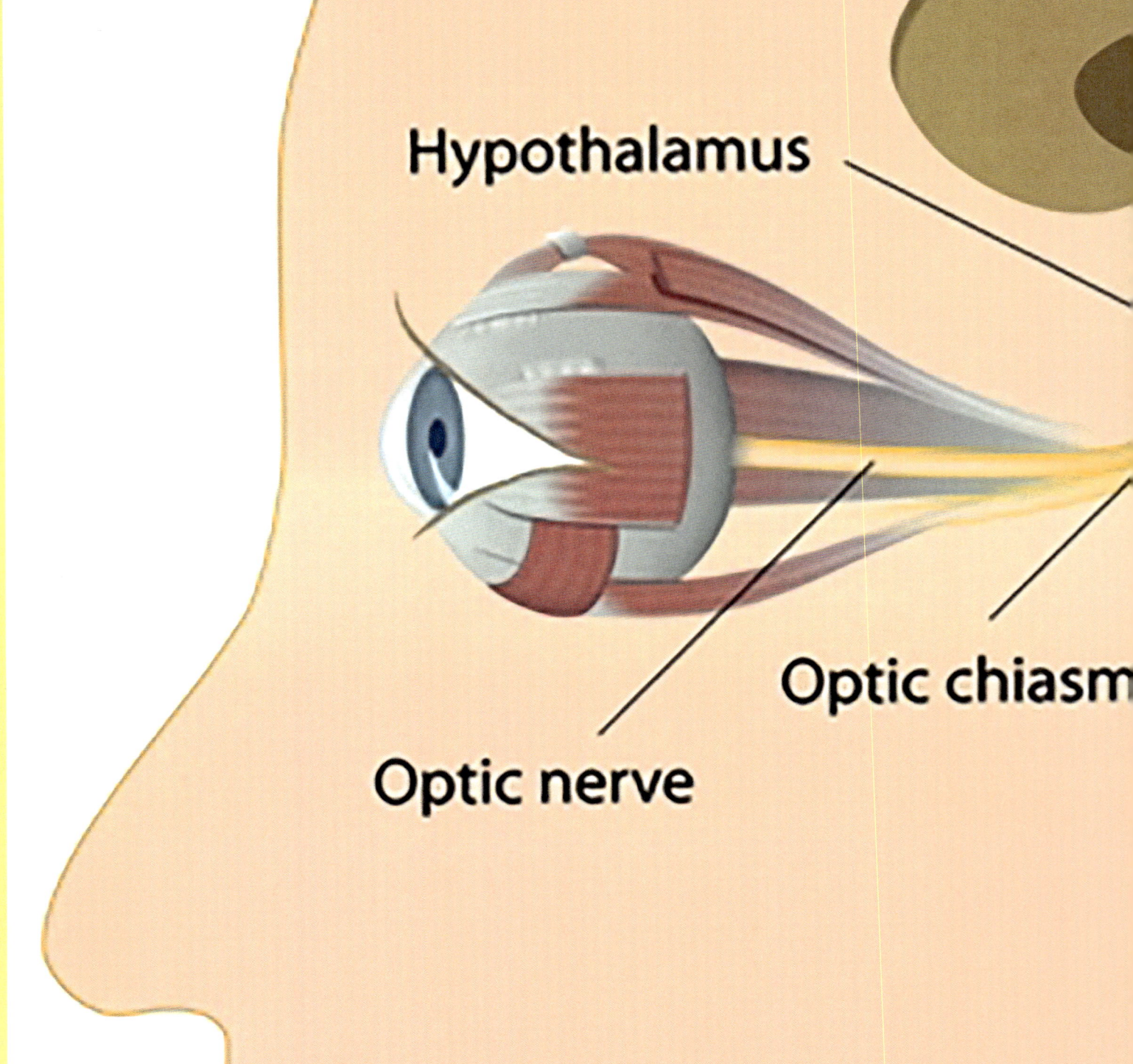

THE OPTIC NERVE

The cells of the retina, both rods and cones, transform the colors, tints, and contrasts you see into electrical signals. These signals, which are messages sent through your nerves, travel along the optic nerve to your brain so you can figure out what you're seeing. In addition to interpreting what you are seeing, your brain helps control how your eye focuses and where it is looking. Both eyes work smoothly together so that we can see.

PROTECT YOUR EYES

Your eyes are really important. Make sure to wear goggles to protect your eyes if you do woodworking or other hobbies where metals, woods, or chemicals could cause your eyes damage.

You should wear eye protection when you're playing sports that might hurt your eyes too. UV light can damage your eyes as well, so wear good quality sunglasses so you won't get cataracts when you get older. Cataracts make the lenses in your eyes murky so you can't see as well.

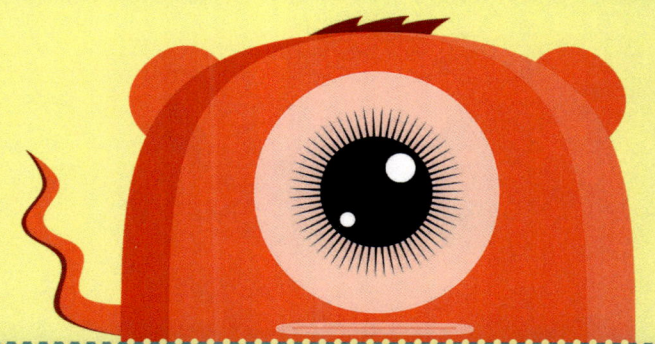

Awesome! Now you know more about your amazing sense of sight and the process of how your eyes see. You can find more Biology books from Baby Professor by searching the website of your favorite book retailer.

Made in the USA
Las Vegas, NV
17 April 2021